transition
solace and comfort for the broken hearted

Charlotte D. Grant-Cobb, PhD

Copyright © 2014 by Charlotte D. Grant-Cobb, PhD

Published by RICHER Press

4600 E. Washington Street, Suite 300
Phoenix, Arizona 85034
www.richerlifellc.com

All rights reserved. No portion of this publication may be reproduced, stored in a retrieval system, or transmitted in any form by any means-except for brief quotations in printed reviews-without the prior written permission of the publisher.

Richer Press books and products are available through most bookstores. RICHER Press also publishes its books in a variety of electronic formats. Some content that appears in print may not be available in electronic books.

Scripture quotations are taken from the Holy Bible are from New International Version

© 1973, 1978, 1984, 2011, Biblica®

All quotations without attribution are assumed to be anonymous.

Library of Congress Cataloging-in-Publications Data
Charlotte D. Grant-Cobb, PhD

Transition
Solace and Comfort for the Broken Hearted

Charlotte D. Grant-Cobb, PhD – 1st edition p. cm

1. Inspiration   2. Self Help   3. Spiritual

ISBN : 978-0-9903291-8-3

Printed in the United States of America

Printed in the

United States of America

First Edition, 2014

A Gift For:

_____

From:

_____

solace and comfort for the broken hearted

For the one who is giving this gift

Introduction: *transition*

There is a list that is supposed to represent the most stressful events that may occur in a person's life; they include death of a loved one, loss of a job, being divorced, moving and/or experiencing a health crisis. Understandably, losing a loved one is usually first on the list.

What do you say to someone who has lost a loved one? How do you tell a dear friend how deeply sorry you are for their loss? How can you bring hope to the person that feels guilty because they lived and their loved one died?

I believe that you offer comfort and solace in as many ways as you can. You do say, "I'm so sorry for your loss,' because you are. You do drop off a casserole during the time of bereavement. You do send "hoping you are well" cards, books, letters and songs. You do call and leave a message, even if they don't answer.

I believe that you envelope your friend with love even when they can't feel it or receive it. You do pick up their dry cleaning, or take their children to dinner after soccer practice. You do pick up take-out from their favorite restaurant and drop it off with a hug and a promise that you are here when needed.

I believe that you pray, without ceasing, for your friend's healing - and for yours.

If you do these things, then you are doing what you should do. Now, breathe, heal, and let God do the rest. . .

Agape'

Char

renewal
⇧
opportunity
⇧
recovery

solace and comfort for the broken hearted

FOR THE ONE WHO IS RECEIVING THIS GIFT

INTRODUCTION: *transition*

Hello. Your friend has given you this book to offer you comfort and solace during your time of loss.

Unbelievably, I went through a period of over five years where I lost dear friend, after dear friend. I lost a loved one to a devastating car accident, two dear friends to terminal illnesses, more simply were lost, too soon. Right now as I write this introduction, I miss them, and I always will. I wrote many of the passages in this book after the devastating loss of each dear loved one. The writing process helped me find my way through the period from life with them - to - life without them. I hope that these messages of healing, hope and restoration will reach you, sooth you, and comfort you.

Helping you through that state, from life with them-to-embracing and honoring life without them, is the purpose of this book. Let's start working through that transition right now.

Please know that I understand that you will never "get over" the loss of your loved one. No one here is asking you to do that, and why in the world should you? Whether you had a lot of years with that person, or too few, you made loving memories together.

But I also know ways that you can honor those memories, wrap their love around you like a warm blanket, and still stay open to God's anointed plan for your life. I wrote this book to help you embrace your God-given gifts and to walk out, in a new way, His purpose for your life.

Please know that I understand that the state of transition is not some idyllic place for rest and recuperation. If it were, you would never want to leave that state of mind. There will be days when you just can't stop crying.

There are times when you wake up with every intention to reconnect, and then, regret, guilt or anger will trip you up, and you find yourself right in the path of the hurricane again. There are days when your pain is so great, you want to retreat and hide from the world.

You have to know that you can't stay in this space forever. Deep sorrow is not a place to build a future, raise a family, or fulfill God's purpose for your life.

Dry your tears for just a few moments at a time, so that you can see the breaking of day! Suddenly, you are standing in the silver-calm eye of the storm. This is where you can look up, and look out, and look forward.

Opportunities for recovery are iterative. When you can feel okay for a day, trust that you will feel okay for two days-then for three days, and on and on. When you can feel okay, that means you can feel better. And when you start to feel better, you will feel good again.

Solace is only a prayer away. Prayer and active mediation will connect you physically and spiritually with a power greater than you. You will find comfort and strength by combining physical movement with your prayer and recover.

Transition enables recovery. Recovery uncovers opportunities to move from mourning to dancing, from guilt to forgiveness, from loss to renewal.

I share this book of encouragements with you, in no sequential order; because, some days you will feel great and energized, and on other days, you can't stop crying. This book is my way of honoring the gifts of your loved one. Those gifts are still here with you, in the memories you share, and in the plans you made. I hope that a word or phrase will support you during your season of transition.

I dispatch these words to you, through the authority that comes from serving the one true and living God, Jehovah, and his son, Christ Jesus. In this walk, I have found a peace that surpasses all understanding. May you find that same blessed Peace.

Agape'

Char

solace and comfort for the broken hearted

I cannot understand the why
I just know I miss you

I do cherish our
life together

I have strength to
move through and
over any obstacles

I move without hesitation
toward God's promise for me

solace and comfort for the broken hearted

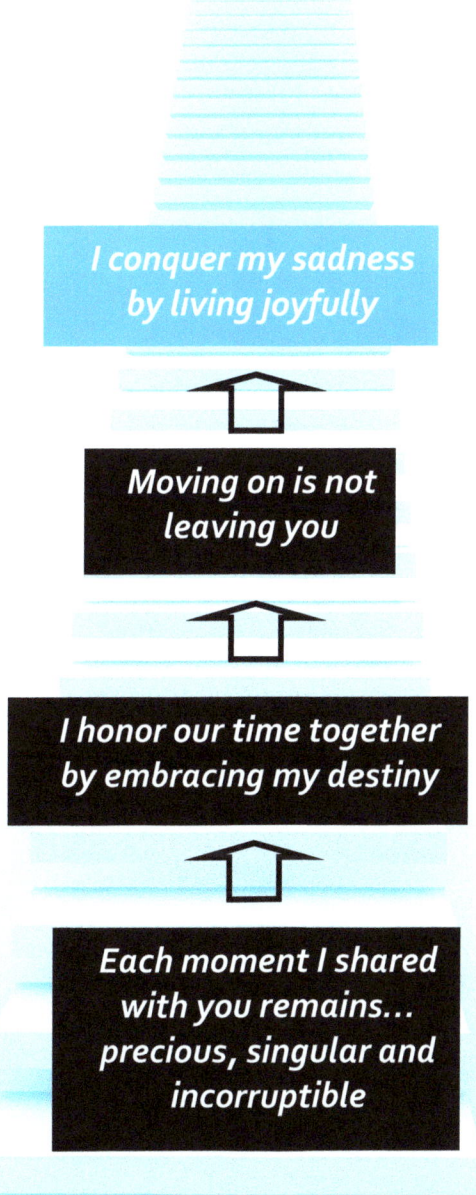

solace and comfort for the broken hearted

I trust this new day
Lead the way

Thanks for staying
I'm okay

I think of you every day, in so many ways and so often
that you might as well be a phone call away
Hello

I feel the warmth of your spirit when I
welcome the morning sun

I am lifted beyond my grief
I am buoyed by my knowledge that
you have at last found peace

solace and comfort for the broken hearted

opportunity

There is simply no room for despair

Light breaks through this dark time to remind me of hope and joy shared

I am taking it step by step, day by day

I am one with you
The music I hear in my heart is the songs we sang each day

I seek new opportunities because your strength is always with me

solace and comfort for the broken hearted

Psalm 30: 6-12

6 When I felt secure, I said,
"I will never be shaken."
7 LORD, when you favored me,
you made my royal mountain stand firm;
but when you hid your face,
I was dismayed.
8 To you, LORD, I called;
to the Lord I cried for mercy:
9 "What is gained if I am silenced,
if I go down to the pit?
Will the dust praise you?
Will it proclaim your faithfulness?
10 Hear, LORD, and be merciful to me;
LORD, be my help."
11 You turned my wailing into dancing;
you removed my sackcloth and clothed me with joy,
12 that my heart may sing your praises and not be silent

solace and comfort for the broken hearted

Psalms 25: 4 - 5

4 Show me your ways, LORD,

teach me your paths.

5 Guide me in your truth and teach me,

for you are God my Savior,

and my hope is in you all day long.

You showed me the way, so I will not veer from that path

solace and comfort for the broken hearted

You can never be replaced but I can share your gifts with the world

I remember you and I'll never forget - any of it

I am the gift you wrapped for the world

Today I refresh our shared dreams with new visions and ideas

I stay encouraged so I can finish the work we started

solace and comfort for the broken hearted

Psalm 25:23 NIV

23 "His master replied, Well done, good and faithful servant! You have been faithful with a few things; I will put you in charge of many things. Come and share your master's happiness!"

solace and comfort for the broken hearted

My heart beats and I am hopeful

I know you are with me in each kiss of the wind
each drop of rain
each tear I shed

The universe is filled with possibilities
and I am supported in this journey

I know renewal will come,
but I will miss you always

solace and comfort for the broken hearted

I am able to still my mind
experience your transition and
not lose myself

Your gift of pure love is
still the best part of me

I will activate my body
mind and spirit to awaken the promise
you saw in me

Today, I'm going to allow
myself to ache for you

solace and comfort for the broken hearted

Come Holy Spirit
Comfort me
Support me
Guide me

Today I will be the person you trusted me to become

I embrace every good reminder of you

I take into me a peace that surpasses all understanding and give thanks to the Lord

solace and comfort for the broken hearted

Your friendship still supports me

My life is still full of promise and questions unasked

I wake to a new day to embrace the joy of our time together

Peace and calm are my guides today

solace and comfort for the broken hearted

*Because you shared your life with me
I can share my life with others*

*I rest knowing you are with
God and God is with me*

*I awake to share your message your
dreams and your plans with our friends*

*I am amazed by God's grace even
when I don't understand this loss*

solace and comfort for the broken hearted

Even when I breakdown from missing you
a smile is not far behind

I count it all joy to know the goodness
mercy and glory of the Lord

Our time together was precious
I am better for it

I may have missed our last goodbye
but you are here in each new hello

solace and comfort for the broken hearted

Psalms 118:24

24 This is the day which the LORD hath made;
We will rejoice and be glad in it.

solace and comfort for the broken hearted

I am so glad I have the writings
and words you left for me
Thank you

⬆

I still rest knowing you are with
God and God is with me

⬆

I know this
God is God
and I am not

⬆

I can let go without forgetting

solace and comfort for the broken hearted

No one could keep the family together like you
We're hanging in there but it's not the same

I treat every penny that I find on the ground as a greeting from you
I love it when you say "hi"

We called you the General and you better believe, your absence left a space in the universe that no one else can fill

When I see a painting, riotous with color and images, I see you

solace and comfort for the broken hearted

The rivers miss you
the ski slopes miss you
the golf courses miss you
I miss you

You were moving so fast near the end trying to grab all the life that life had to offer
I will live full-out too

Miss you so much my friend

I can't hear an Irish jig without thinking of you

solace and comfort for the broken hearted

I am turning the next page

My transition has ended

I move with confidence toward the zest of my life
I move with confidence toward the rest of life

Someone is waiting for me to arrive

solace and comfort for the broken hearted

I cherish yesterday today and tomorrow

I am stepping into the changes that I need to make

I embrace the grace peace and calm that comes to me through faith

I send you grace and peace for your journey

solace and comfort for the broken hearted

I'm so glad we shared precious dreams; find me if I move off course

solace and comfort for the broken hearted

Romans 8: 26-28

26 In the same way, the Spirit helps us in our weakness. We do not know what we ought to pray for, but the Spirit himself intercedes for us through wordless groans. 27 And he who searches our hearts knows the mind of the Spirit, because the Spirit intercedes for God's people in accordance with the will of God.

28 And we know that in all things God works for the good of those who love him, who [i] have been called according to his purpose.

solace and comfort for the broken hearted

About the Author

Charlotte Grant-Cobb uses her gifts to develop affirmations for those who desire to create new habits, new pathways. . . new experiences.